THE NEW BABY

This book is about

_____

Prepared, with love, by

_____

OTHER GIFTBOOKS BY HELEN EXLEY:

The Baby Blessing
My Wedding Planner
A Christening Gift
Brothers...
Sisters...

Thoughts on... Being a Mother
Wedding Guest Book
Welcome to the New Baby

To a very special Daughter
To a very special Son
Dads...

To a very special Granddaughter
To a very special Grandson
For a wonderful Grandchild
For a beautiful Daughter

12 11 10 9 8 7

Published simultaneously in 1993 by Exley Publications Ltd
in Great Britain and Exley Publications LLC in the USA.

Copyright © Helen Exley 1993
The moral right of the author has been asserted.

ISBN 1-85015-445-7

A copy of the CIP data is available from the British Library on request.

Edited and pictures selected by Helen Exley.
Border illustrations by Maria Teresa Meloni.
Printed in China.

Exley Publications Ltd, 16 Chalk Hill, Watford, Herts WD19 4BG, UK.
Exley Publications LLC, 185 Main Street, Spencer, MA 01562 USA.
www.helenexleygiftbooks.com

IMPORTANT NOTE
For best results we recommend that you use a fountain pen, marker or a felt tip
to fill in this book. The pressure of a ball point pen will show through and spoil
the following pages.

Our Baby's Record Book

A HELEN EXLEY GIFTBOOK

EXLEY

INTRODUCTION

Here is a journal that enables you to keep a record of some of the most amazing and joyful experiences in life – the first weeks and years of a child's existence!

Write down the events as they occur: all those happy, chaotic and hilarious moments. Then, later on, you will be able to focus on this time in your life and relive it all with a smile. Babies are babies for such a short time. Enjoy it and remember to record everything. This book will make a precious memento for both you and your child – and perhaps, one day, even for your grandchildren.

It doesn't matter how beautiful the pictures in this book are, your pictures of your baby and the incidents in your life are far more precious. Glue in lots of photographs and your child's first drawings. Rewrite headings so that they're relevant to you – make this book your own.

HELEN EXLEY

IMPORTANT NOTE:
For best results we recommend that you use a fountain pen, a marker or a felt tip to fill in this book. The pressure of a ball point pen will show through and spoil the following pages.

CONTENTS

THE BIRTH

PLACE

DATE   TIME

WEIGHT   LENGTH

WHAT YOU LOOKED LIKE

THINGS WE WILL NEVER FORGET

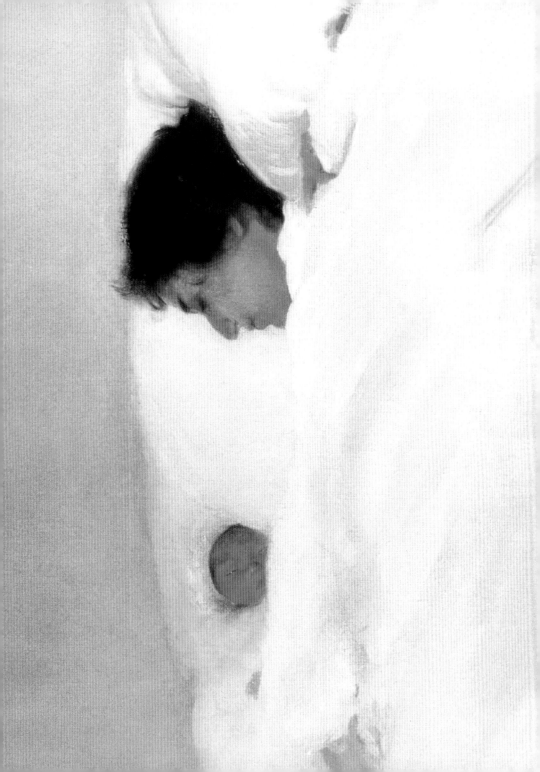

FIRST VISITORS

WHAT THEY SAID ABOUT YOU

MESSAGES, GIFTS AND FLOWERS

A SPACE FOR A CARD, MEMENTO OR PHOTOGRAPH

WHAT YOUR ARRIVAL MEANT TO US

FAMILY TREE

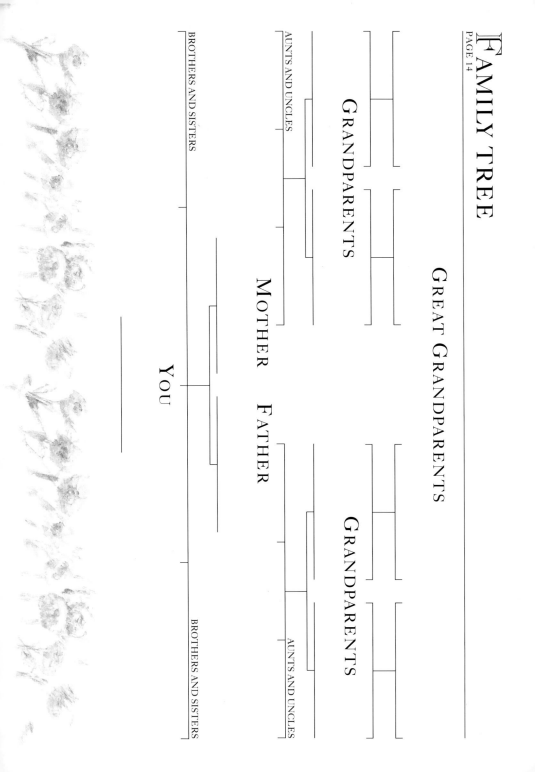

GREAT GRANDPARENTS

GRANDPARENTS

GRANDPARENTS

AUNTS AND UNCLES

AUNTS AND UNCLES

MOTHER

FATHER

BROTHERS AND SISTERS

BROTHERS AND SISTERS

YOU

IMPORTANT RELATIVES AND FAMILY FRIENDS

SOME FAMILY HISTORY

WHO THEY WERE AND WHAT THEY DID

HOW YOUR PARENTS MET

YOUR MOTHER

HER EARLY LIFE, HOW YOUR COMING CHANGED HER LIFE,
HER DREAMS AND HOPES FOR YOU.

HER MESSAGE TO YOU

FOR A PHOTO OF MOTHER

YOUR FATHER

SOMETHING ABOUT HIS LIFE BEFORE YOU CAME, WHAT YOUR COMING MEANT TO HIM
WHAT HE HOPES FOR YOU.

A MESSAGE TO KEEP

FOR A PHOTO OF DAD

FOR PHOTOGRAPHS OR MEMENTOS

Your Grandparents – A Little of Their Lives

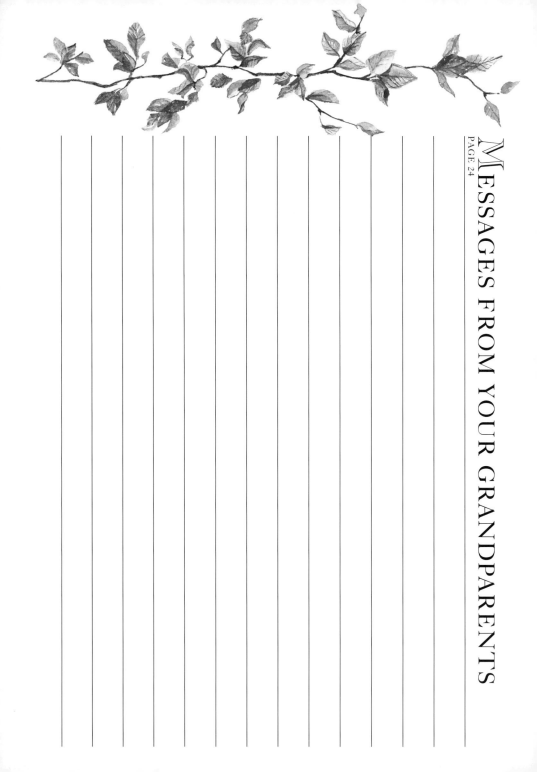

MESSAGES FROM YOUR GRANDPARENTS

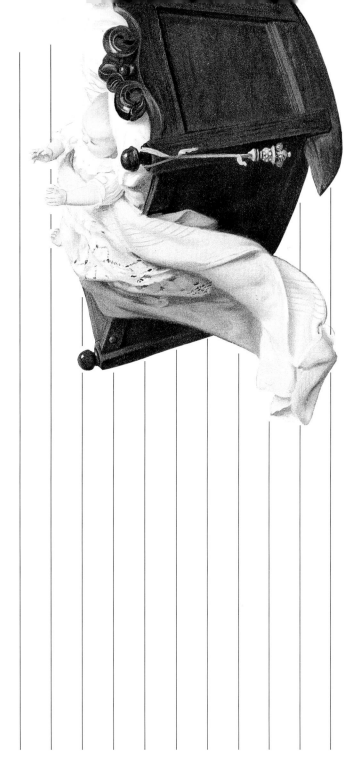

YOUR ROOM

THE WORLD AS IT WAS WHEN YOU WERE BORN

PRESS CLIPPINGS, INSTEAD OF PHOTOGRAPHS, COULD BE ADDED HERE OR TO ANY OF THE PAGES IN THIS BOOK.

FUNNY MOMENTS

FIRSTS IN THE EARLY MONTHS

GRASPED A FINGER

HELD HEAD UP

RECOGNIZED A PARENT'S VOICE

RECOGNIZED YOUR OWN NAME

SMILED

DISCOVERED YOUR OWN HANDS

SUCKED YOUR THUMB

ATE SOLID FOODS

MEMENTOS
PAGE 35

YOUR HAND PRINT

YOUR FOOTPRINT

A LOCK OF HAIR

DON'T FORGET THE DATES!

THINGS TO REMEMBER

JOYS AND SADNESSES, EXCITEMENTS AND DISCOVERIES.

FOR MEMENTOS OR PHOTOGRAPHS

OUTINGS

PLACES YOU WENT

FIRST VISITS TO RELATIVES, THE SEA, THE FOREST, A FAIRGROUND...

PLACES AND THINGS THAT DELIGHTED YOU

TIMES WHEN IT ALL WENT WRONG!

YOUR BEST-LOVED THINGS

PEOPLE, TOYS, SONGS, RHYMES, MUSIC – ANYTHING AND EVERYTHING

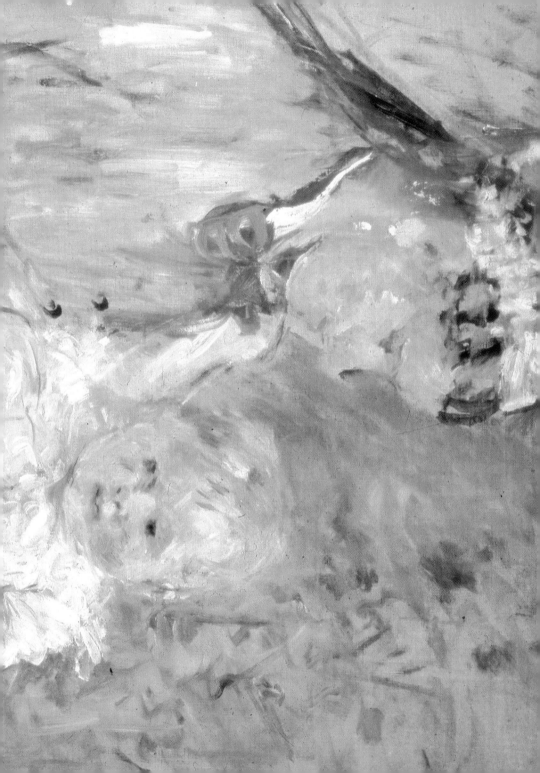

GROWTH CHART

AGE	HEIGHT	WEIGHT
ONE WEEK		
ONE MONTH		
TWO MONTHS		
THREE MONTHS		
SIX MONTHS		
ONE YEAR		
EIGHTEEN MONTHS		
TWO YEARS		
THREE YEARS		
FOUR YEARS		
FIVE YEARS		

TOOTH CHART

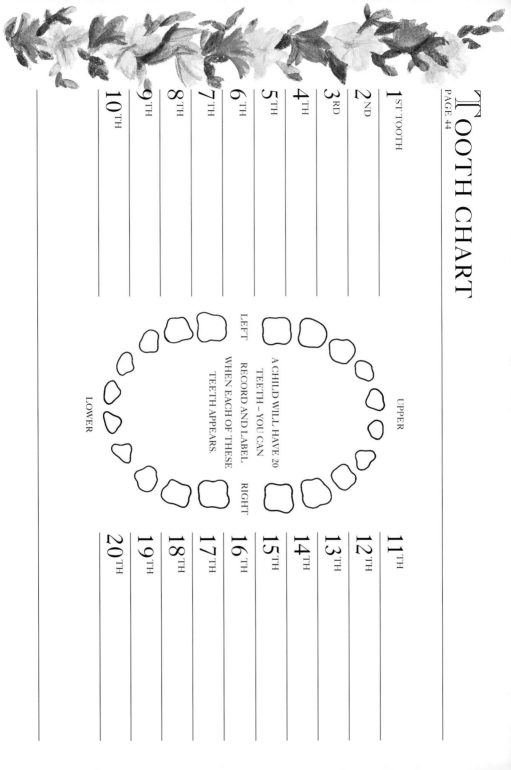

1 ST TOOTH

2 ND

3 RD

4 TH

5 TH

6 TH

7 TH

8 TH

9 TH

10 TH

UPPER

LEFT

A CHILD WILL HAVE 20
TEETH – YOU CAN
RECORD AND LABEL
WHEN EACH OF THESE
TEETH APPEARS.

RIGHT

LOWER

11 TH

12 TH

13 TH

14 TH

15 TH

16 TH

17 TH

18 TH

19 TH

20 TH

MEDICAL RECORDS

DATE

DOCTOR'S VISITS

ILLNESSES

ALLERGIES

BLOOD GROUP

OTHER IMPORTANT INFORMATION

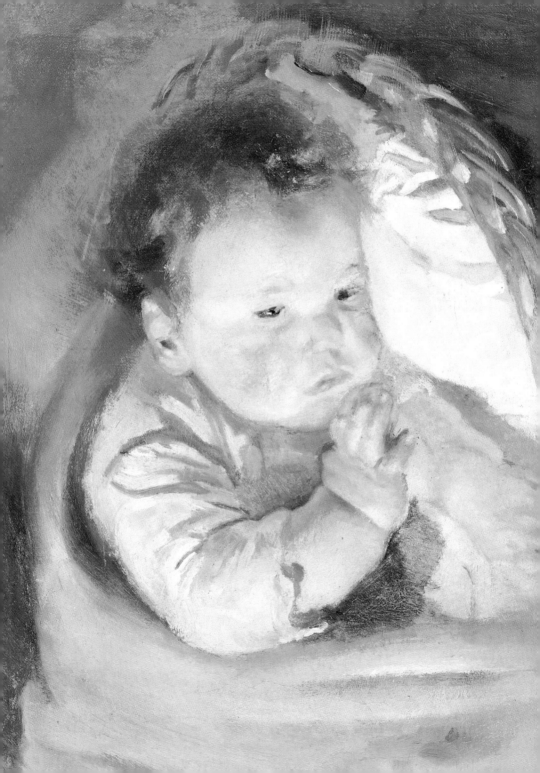

IMMUNIZATIONS

VERY IMPORTANT! KEEP ACCURATE DETAILS FOR FUTURE REFERENCE.

IMMUNIZATION	DATE
MEASLES	
POLIO	
TETANUS	
WHOOPING COUGH	
OTHERS	

ONE VERY SPECIAL DAY

FOR A CHRISTENING OR NAMING DAY, OR AN IMPORTANT HAPPY DAY FOR THE FAMILY.

YOUR FIRST LONGER JOURNEYS

VISITS TO GRANDPARENTS, WEEKEND TRIPS, OVERSEAS TRAVEL...

CELEBRATIONS! FESTIVALS! PARTIES! FUN!

OUR FAMILY
PAGE 57

TRADITIONS, WHAT WE ARE LIKE, WHAT WE DO, WHAT WE ENJOY.

MORE MILESTONES

FIRST LAUGHED OUT LOUD

FIRST WAVED BYE-BYE

FIRST RECOGNIZED YOURSELF IN THE MIRROR

FIRST PRESS-UP

FIRST ROLLED OVER

FIRST CRAWLED

FIRST SAT UP UNSUPPORTED

OTHER IMPORTANT FIRSTS

FIRST SOUNDS AND WORDS

RECORDING THE DATES COULD BE IMPORTANT, TOO.

ONE YEAR OLD

AFTER ONE YEAR – THE THINGS YOU MOST LOVED

STORIES, SONGS, GAMES, FRIENDS...

A TYPICAL DAY

AND LITTLE THINGS WE LOVED DOING TOGETHER.

MILESTONES AS YOU GREW

THE WORST TIMES

THINGS THAT FRIGHTENED YOU

THINGS YOU HATED

ACCIDENTS AND DISASTERS

SAD EVENTS

YOUR FIRST MISCHIEF – AND PUNISHMENT

TALENTS AND INTERESTS AS YOU GREW

EARLY DRAWINGS

GLUE THE BEST EXAMPLES HERE AND ON THE MEMENTO PAGES.

FIRST SCHOOL-DAYS

YOUR FIRST DAY

YOUR TEACHERS

SUBJECTS YOU LOVED

SUBJECTS YOU HATED

OTHER IMPORTANT THINGS IN SCHOOL

YOUR EARLY HOPES AND AMBITIONS

EARLY GOALS AND DREAMS

ACHIEVEMENTS

DIFFICULTIES YOU OVERCAME

IMPORTANT EVENTS OF YOUR CHILDHOOD

THE THINGS YOU SAID!

ALL SMALL CHILDREN COME OUT WITH DELIGHTFUL, WISE, FUNNY OR OUTRAGEOUS THINGS – HERE ARE SOME OF YOURS.

FOR A DRAWING OR PIECE OF WRITING

THINGS WE'LL ALWAYS REMEMBER

PARENTS, GRANDPARENTS AND PEOPLE WHO LOVE YOU COULD WRITE MEMORIES AND MESSAGES HERE.

ACKNOWLEDGEMENTS

FRONT COVER
Motherhood, 1898, Louis Adan (1839-1937), The Bridgeman Art Library.

PAGE 4
Oestliche Landschaft, Karl Bantzer b. 1857, Archiv für Kunst, Berlin.

PAGE 9
Mother, Joaquin y Bastida Sorolla (1863-1923), Museo Sorolla, Madrid, The Bridgeman Art Library.

PAGE 13
Mutter und Kind, Bernd Lehmann b. 1952, Archiv für Kunst.

PAGE 16
Rockabye Baby, Jane M. Dealey (flourished 1880-1930), Fine Art Photographic Library Ltd.

PAGE 25
After the Battle, Angus Macdonnall b.1876, Forbes Magazine Collection, New York, The Bridgeman Art Library.

PAGE 27
Mother's Darling, Arthur John Elsey (1861-1952), Fine Art Photographic Library Ltd.

PAGE 31
The Beautiful Baby Competition, Sir Frank Brangwyn (1867-1956), Bonhams London, The Bridgeman Art Library.

PAGE 33
Der Stammhalter, L.A. Tessier, Archiv für Kunst/Image Select.

PAGE 34
Le Berceau, Berthe Morisot (1841-1895), Musée d'Orsay, Paris, Archiv für Kunst/Image Select.

PAGE 39
The Forest of Paris, Julius Melchern, Musée d'Orsay, Paris, Art Resource, New York.

PAGE 41
A Watchful Eye, Viggo Pedersen, Christies Colour Library.

PAGE 42
Juliet Manet and Her Nurse, Berthe Morisot (1841-1895), Private Collection, The Bridgeman Art Library.

PAGE 45
Mother and Child, Wilfred Fairclough b.1907, Warrington Museum and Art Gallery Lancs, The Bridgeman Art Library.

PAGE 47
Bimbo in Culla, Armando Spadini (1883-1925), Museo Civico Piacenza, Scala.

PAGE 49
L'anno 1918 a Pietrogrado, Kuzma Petrov-Vodkin (1878-1939), Tret'jakov Gallery, Moscow, Scala.

PAGE 51
Chris Beetles Gallery, London.